# A GUIDEBOOK TO LIGHTHOUSES IN NORTH AND SOUTH CAROLINA, GEORGIA, AND FLORIDA'S EAST COAST

## RUDY KAGERER

LIGHTHOUSE ENTERPRISES, INC.
ATHENS, GEORGIA

First Edition, November,1996- Revised, June,1998
Copyright (c) 1998 by Rudy Kagerer
All Rights Reserved

Library of Congress Cataloging-in-Publication-Data
ISBN 0-933549-01-6

Price per copy: $9.95

Lighthouse Enterprises, Inc.
P.O. Box 6361
Athens, Georgia 30604

Cover Photo: Doris Kagerer in front of St. Simons Island Lighthouse.
All photos by Rudy Kagerer except where noted.

TO

DORIS EMMA KAGERER,

My Wife, Partner, and Best Friend

ERIC, VICKIE , DANNY AND SUSAN,
(Our sons and their wives.)

AND

JASON, CHRISTOPHER AND MELISSA,
(The Newest Generation)

# THE LIGHTHOUSE KEEPER'S LAMENT

Oh, what is the bane of a lightkeeper's life,
That causes him worry and struggle and strife,
That makes him use cuss words and beat at his wife?
    **It's Brasswork.**
The devil himself could never invent
A material causing more world-wide lament,
And in Uncle Sam's service about ninety percent,
    **Is Brasswork.**
The lamp in the tower, reflector and shade,
The tools and accessories pass in parade,
As a matter of fact the whole outfit is made,
    **Of Brasswork.**
From pillar to post, rags and polish I tote,
I'm never without them, for you will please note
That even the buttons I wear on my coat,
    **Are Brasswork.**
I dig, scrub and polish, and work with a might,
And just when I get it all shiny and bright,
In comes the fog like a thief in the night.
    **Goodbye Brasswork.**
Oh, why should the spirit of mortal be proud,
In the short span of life that he is allowed,
If all of the lining in every dark cloud,
    **Is Brasswork?**
And when I have polished until I am cold,
And I'm taken aloft in the Heavenly fold,
Will my harp and my crown be made of pure gold?
    **No, Brasswork.**

                Anonymous

# TABLE OF CONTENTS

Note: There are nine other lighthouses along this coast. Six of them are off the coast of the Florida Keys, and are well described in Love Dean's book, "Reef Lights: Seaswept Lighthouses of the Florida Keys", by the Historic Key West Preservation Board, 1982.

The other three are offshore lights of the texas tower type at Diamond Shoals, Frying Pan Shoals, and the Savannah light off Tybee Island.

These were not included in this volume because of the difficulties involved in reaching them, as well as the restricted acess to them.

# INTRODUCTION

A book of this sort takes the combined effort of a lot of people. I would like to express my appreciation to all those who bought and read my first effort, which included the lighthouses of South Carolina, Georgia, and Florida's East Coast. The wonderful lighthouses of North Carolina have been added to this edition to provide total coverage of the southeastern coast. I have,in addition corrected some errors made in the first book. I hope I learned by my mistakes.

Members of the U.S. Coast Guard have been especially helpful to this volume, including several who shared pictures and information about those lighthouses in their area. The many volunteers at the lighthouse museums were also of great help. Their enthusiasm and dedication have done much to save some of our lighthouses from falling into ruin. Those are the "good news" structures. There are still a few "bad news" lighthouses that have not been adopted, but there is hope.

A word of caution is in order. If you are going to visit some of the more remote sites, take the following precautions: Never go alone. When you do venture to a remote site, notify someone; a park ranger, a law enforcement official, or someone you can trust, of your destination and expected time of return. If going by boat, be prepared for changes in wind, weather and tides. Bring a compass, fresh water, emergency food, a flashlight, and/or other supplies that may be needed if you become stranded. Also, access to lighthouses is not always automatic. Some are in protected areas.

Others have specific hours of operation. Check these, and make arrangements where necessary. Neither I nor the publisher can be held responsible for any incidents that may occur in your search for lighthouses.

I am grateful to my friends and family for their support. I am particularly blessed with a patient and supportive wife, Doris, who has accompanied me on many of my wild lighthouse searches, eating lunches on windswept beaches, and walking long distances in soft beach sand to get the "right" picture. I have the good fortune to have, as my wife, the finest woman "from Rabun Gap to the Tybee light", to steal a quote from the poet Sydney Lanier

Those who are further interested in these and other lighthouses are invited to become a part of one or more of the lighthouse support groups listed later in this book. There is a representative list of readings and a glossary of terms to help you become acquainted with the romance and mystery of our coastal sentinels. Where there is room, you will find some poems at the end of some of the units. Enjoy them.

My fond hope is that some of you who read this book will use it to seek out these exciting places, and have the experience of climbing stairs, finding sites, walking beaches, riding boats, and in general becoming a part of the great coastal heritage that is represented by our remaining lighthouses.

I am fully responsible for the content of this book. The opinions expressed are solely mine, and the research is also mine. If I have misstated any fact, I am sorry. I will correct any error that I am made aware of.

Welcome to the world of "wickies".

Athens, Georgia 1996                    Rudy Kagerer

# A BRIEF HISTORY OF AMERICA'S LIGHTHOUSES

The earliest lighthouses built on American soil were built on the coasts of the maritime powers of the original colonies. These coastal lights were built and controlled locally, some by business interests and others by local authorities. They were supported by a tonnage tax levied on all ships entering or leaving the ports they protected. The lights were the responsibility of local contractors who maintained the structures, hired and paid keepers, supplied oil and necessities, all at a contracted price. These lights were not always dependable, and, in fact, many were not lit in foul weather, since the poorly paid keepers chose not to expose themselves to the wet and cold.

While there is some indication that the Spanish had built a daymark on Fernandina Island near Saint Augustine, Florida, the first fully functioning lighthouse of record was built in Boston Harbor in 1716, with ten more to be added by the time of independence.

When the Federal Government took over the responsibility for the navigational aids system in 1789, two more major lights were added, bringing the total to thirteen, and four more were under construction.

As the country grew, lighthouses were being built on major waterways as well as on both coasts. The Gulf Coast lights began with Franks Island in 1818, the Great Lakes system in 1819 with Presque Isle, and on the West Coast , under pressure from gold seekers, Alcatraz Island lighthouse was built in 1854. The Russian built lighthouse at Sitka became Board responsibility in 1867 when the U.S. took possession of "Seward's Folly", but no further structures were built until 1902. Thirteen active Spanish-built lighthouses were absorbed in 1900, when Puerto Rico became a territory of the U.S. The Board assumed responsibility for Hawaii's lights in 1904, and for the five lighthouses in the American Virgin Islands in 1919.

Administration of lighthouses bounced around somewhat for over thirty years after 1789, going from Treasury to Commerce to Commissioner of Revenue, back to Treasury, etc. until 1822, when the aids to navigation was placed in the Treasury Department, with the Fifth Auditor of the Treasury, Mr. Stephen Plimpton in charge. He was a conscientious, hard working civil servant. He did, however, have two faults. He knew little of the technical aspects of lighthouses, and was extremely frugal with taxpayer money (an attitude we might find desirable in some parts of our government today). The net result of these factors was that the lighthouse system in the U.S. lagged behind those in the more settled countries, particularly in Europe. Many lights were undependable and poorly lit. While Europe began installing the fresnel lens soon after its invention in 1822, Mr. Plimpton finally sent a representative to Europe in 1842, to study the lights and bring two back to determine their utility. They were installed in the Twin Lights in Navesink, New Jersey.

In 1852 the Lighthouse Board was formed. It consisted of naval officers and technical experts. The Board worked hard to bring the system up to world standards, and succeeded in great part. However, political patronage interfered, in that keepers were political appointees, and many had neither talent nor dedication for the job. In 1898, President Grover Cleveland had the Civil Service Laws amended to include keepers and other members of the service. This was the birth of the true lighthouse keepers.

2

In 1910 the Lighthouse Board was replaced by the Bureau of Lighthouses, within the Department of Commerce. There was now one commissioner, a Mr. George R. Putnam, who served as Bureau Commissioner from 1910 until his retirement in 1935. Mr. Putnam truly modernized the navigational aids in the United States during this period. If he had one fault, it was that such emphasis was placed on thrift, that some necessary maintenance was not performed on many of the aids to navigation. This is a situation that often reoccurs today, as the money needed to keep up some of the current aids to navigation is not always available in times of shrinking budgets.

In 1939, just prior to the 150th anniversary of federal involvement in lighthouses, President Franklin D. Roosevelt abolished the Bureau of Lighthouses, and placed responsibility for all navigational aids with the Coast Guard, where it currently resides.

As of this writing, there may be one lighthouse keeper in the old style left, but that will change when he retires. The lighthouses that are operating are almost all automated. The families that lived in the lonesome sites are gone. The gas powered argon lamps have been replaced by powerful electric lamps, mounted three or four to a device that automatically rotates to a new lamp when one burns out.

BUT, the romance of lighthouses lives on in our hearts and in our minds. They still stand in awesome splendor to remind us of our treasured past, and to give us a small taste of what it was like. Let's go find out a little about them, shall we?

Virginia

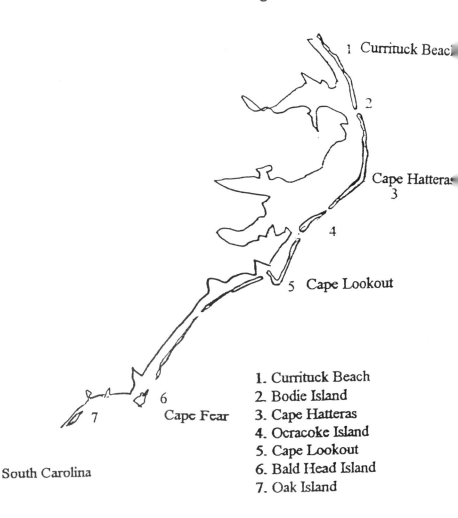

1. Currituck Beach
2. Bodie Island
3. Cape Hatteras
4. Ocracoke Island
5. Cape Lookout
6. Bald Head Island
7. Oak Island

NORTH CAROLINA

4

## CURRITUCK BEACH, COROLLA, N.C.

**HISTORY.** During the lighthouse building activity on the east coast in the mid to late 1800's, there was an 80 mile long "dark spot" between the Cape Henry and Bodie Island lighthouses. This void was filled in the winter of 1875, when the Currituck Beach lighthouse, lying about halfway between the two, was first lit.

The lens is a first order fresnel, lit initially by a mineral oil lamp, with five concentric wicks. The tower, left a natural reddish brick color, is 158 feet to the focal plane of the lens. It was built with approximately 1 million bricks, and has 214 steps to the top. The lighthouse signature is a 20-second flash cycle: 3 seconds on, 17 seconds off. It can be seen for 18 nautical miles.

**MUSEUM OR INTERPRETIVE SERVICE.** This is a lucky lighthouse. In 1980, a local group, Outer Banks Conservationists, Inc. leased the grounds from the state to restore the outbuildings, and the lighthouse. The grounds and lighthouse are open to visitors daily from 10 a.m. to 6 p.m. from Easter to Thanksgiving. There is a $4.00 fee for admission to both. Information can be obtained by writing:

5

Outer Banks Conservationists, Inc.
P.O. Box 361
Corolla, N.C. 27927

**GETTING THERE.** From US 158 north of Kitty Hawk
take the road toward Duck (NC 12). As you near the
lighthouse, on the left toward Currituck Sound, bear
left, and follow "your nose" to the lighthouse.

**TALES AND LEGENDS.** None now known.

## THE LIGHTHOUSE (1934)

It knows no lands, no flags, no kings
These are inconsequential things,
The one important thing tonight, That every seaman, black
or white, Who seeks a harbor sees a light.
We talk about World brotherhood,
But only here we make it good.
We go on building ships of war,
But, God be praised, do one thing more;
We build a lighthouse on the shore.
The lighthouse has no special friends,
No special foes when night descends.
In all the world the only place,
Though statesmen talk and kings embrace.
Where man becomes one common race.

Douglas Malloch in The San Francisco Chronicle
(from " the Keepers Log", Fall, 1984)

# BODIE ISLAND LIGHT

**HISTORY.** Prior to the building of the Bodie Island Light, 150 miles of coast between Cape Henry, Va. and Cape Hatteras,N.C. were without a lighthouse. In 1837 Lieutenant Napoleon L. Coste of the revenue cutter Campbell examined the coast in that area seeking a location for a lighthouse. He determined that a light was needed on or near Bodie Island so that ships could fix their position for navigating Cape Hatteras, without the need of entering the Gulf Stream. Actual construction began in 1847 by Francis Gibbons, who later became prominent as the builder of lighthouses on the rugged West Coast. Thomas Blount, a former Customs official, was engaged as the project overseer. Blount was quite technically incompetent at lighthouse construction, and, over Gibbons' objections, had an unsupported brick foundation laid, leading to severe leaning and abandonment a mere 12 years later.

The second lighthouse was properly built in 1859, only to be destroyed by Confederate troops two years later. The current tower, with a first order fresnel lens, was first lit on October 1, 1872. Early problems with flocks of geese and lightning strikes were solved with screening and a lightning rod. The light was electrified in 1932, and the property was transferred to the National Park Service in 1953. The tower is 163 feet high, with 214 steps leading to the top.

The light signature is 2.5 seconds on, 2.5 off, 2.5 on, and 22.5 off. The beam can be seen for 18 miles. The daymark design is alternating white and black horizontal stripes, 22 feet wide, topped by a black lantern room and roof.

**GETTING THERE.** This complex is a part of the Cape Hatteras National Seashore. It is located off N.C. 12, 2 miles north of Oregon Inlet.

**MUSEUM.** The keeper's quarters has undergone two renovations since 1953, the latest in 1992. It serves as a museum, gift shop, and visitor center for the lighthouse and for the National Seashore. It is open from Easter or Memorial Day, depending on staffing, to Labor Day, from 9 a.m. to 5 p.m. daily. The lighthouse is not open to visitors.

**TALES AND LEGENDS.** Prior to the operation of the lighthouses on the Outer Banks, wrecking as business was practiced. A lantern was affixed to a mule, and the mule was walked along the beach, luring ships close to land when they saw the bobbing lantern, mistaking it for another ship between them and the shore. The "land pirates" would then plunder the wrecked ship.

Oh! dream of joy!
Is this indeed the ligthouse top I see?
Is this the hill?
Is this the kirk?
Is this mine own countree?

Samuel Coleridge

8

# CAPE HATTERAS LIGHT

**HISTORY.** Cape Hatteras has long been recognized as a hazard to ships. The Gulf Stream from the south and the Labrador Current from the north tend to force ships toward the most dangerous Diamond Shoals, a bar which reaches out eight miles from the Cape. The British Parliament knew about the risk, but showed little interest in building lighthouses in America. Thus nothing was done about the Cape until after the Revolutionary War.

Then, Congress initially ordered the construction of a lighthouse on Cape Hatteras in 1794, but the 95-foot-tower was not lit until 1803.The light was not adequate, so the Board had the tower raised to 150 feet, and fitted it with a first-order Fresnel lens.

At the beginning of the Civil War, Confederates removed the lens and destroyed the light apparatus. It was put back into service in 1862, but mariners still felt it was inadequate. After the war ended, the lighthouse board had a new tower built, with a first-order Fresnel lens. This 208 ft. tower, the tallest in America, has served since October,1871. It's daymark is black and white spiral stripes, with a black lantern room and roof.

The tower was struck by an extraordinary bolt of lightning in 1879, which opened large cracks in its masonry walls, but the tower remained sound. A more serious problem is beach erosion. In 1935 high tides brought the sea to within a few feet of the foundation.

Officials removed the lens and apparatus, placing them on a skeleton tower erected safely inland. The sea reversed itself, and redeposited the beach, so that in 1950 the Coast Guard reactivated the light.

Now, in 1996, the lighthouse is again in danger of being undermined. The sea has again approached to within 150 feet of the tower. The National Park Service has proposed to move the tower inland, but has not received the money or permission to do so. The move is controversial. Some claim that moving such a tower would merely destroy it. It is estimated to weigh 250,000 tons.

**GETTING THERE.** The lighthouse is in Buxton, N.C. just off North Carolina 12, which runs down the Outer Banks. The lighthouse can be seen for miles, and the entrance is clearly marked by a large sign.

**MUSEUM.** The National Park Service operates a museum and gift shop in one of the restored keepers' cottages. The Buxton Visitors Center is open to visitors from 9AM until 5 PM except for Christmas Day. The lighthouse itself is open at specific times for climbing from Easter to Columbus Day. Call to confirm at (919) 995-4474. Admission is free; donations are accepted.

**TALES AND LEGENDS.** None now known.

*The rocky ledge runs far into the sea ,*
*And on its outer point, some miles away,*
*The lighthouse lifts its massive masonry.*
                                        *Longfellow*

## OCRACOKE LIGHT

HISTORY. Ocracoke Inlet has a long history of shipwrecks, the first written record of one being an English ship sunk there in 1585. Following a tower built on Shell Castle Island in 1794, the present structure was built by Noah Porter, a Massachusetts builder, who finished it in 1823 for a total cost of $11,359.00.

In 1854, a fourth-order Fresnel lens was installed to replace the old system. In 1861, a Confederate raid destroyed the lens. A new one was installed by Union forces in 1864. It is the second oldest operating light in the nation, but is an inlet light.

The tower is 75 feet tall, narrowing from 25 feet wide at the base to 12 feet at its peak. It is all white.

GETTING THERE. Ocracoke Island can only be reached by ferry. They sail from Cedar Island and Swan Quarter. Call for reservations (919)225-3551. The cost is $10.00 per car. There is a free state ferry from Hatteras Island to Ocracoke and return.

MUSEUM. The lighthouse can be viewed daily but is not open to the public. The keeper's quarters serve as private residences for park employees. Do not disturb! Interpretive guidance and literature can be obtained from the National Park Service facilities at both the Cape Hatteras and Bodie Island lighthouses. The Visitor's Center, located near the ferry landing, is open from early spring until Labor Day.

**TALES AND LEGENDS.** Early in the eighteenth century, the notorious pirate, Edward Teach, also known as Blackbeard, terrorized ships along the North Carolina Outer Banks, using Ocracoke Island as a convenient anchorage. He was caught there in 1718 by two British sloops under the command of a young Lieutenant Robert Maynard. Outgunning the sloops, the pirates blew the sloops to pieces. Undaunted, Lt. Maynard and his sailors swarmed over the gunwales of Blackbeard's ship, and defeated the pirates in a bloody free-for-all. Blackbeard was one of the pirates to fall in the battle. Legend suggests that the pirate buried some treasure on Ocracoke Island, although none has ever been found, at least not reported.

Eternal granite hewn from the living isle
And dowelled with brute iron,
Rears a tower that from its wet foundation
To its crown of glittering glass,
Stands, in the sweep of winds,
Immovable, immortal, eminent.

Robert Louis Stevenson

# CAPE LOOKOUT LIGHTHOUSE

**HISTORY.** The treacherous 10 mile long shoals that extend off Cape Lookout on Core Banks have long been known to be hazardous to shipping. In early maps Cape Lookout was called *Promontorium Tremendum* or *Horrible Headland.* The original Cape Lookout Lighthouse was completed and lighted in 1812. It was constructed of brick in a wood frame building, and painted red and white horizontal stripes. The 96-foot tower proved inadequate to the task, so a larger one was built.

The present lighthouse was lighted on November 1, 1859. It was made of red brick, stood 163 feet high with a first order fresnel lens. In 1862 Confederate troops damaged the lens and rendered the light useless. A third order lens was installed in 1863, and in 1867 was replaced by the repaired first order lens. The wooden stairs were also replaced with 201 cast iron ones in the same year. In 1873, the new keeper's quarters were completed, and the lighthouse was painted with its distinctive diagonal black and white diamond pattern. The settlement of Diamond City on Shackleford Banks took its name from the design. In 1950 the Cape Lookout Lighthouse was automated. Two airport beacons, each powered with two 1000-watt bulbs produce the light, rotating so as to produce a flash every 15 seconds. The tower base is 28 ft. 7 in. wide, narrowing to 13 ft. 3 in. at the top.

**MUSEUM OR INTERPRETIVE SERVICE.** The Cape Lookout Visitors Center in the keeper's quarters. It is open daily except for Christmas Day.

**GETTING THERE.** Access to Cape Lookout National Seashore is by boat or ferry. There are several ferry services on Harkers Island and in Beaufort. The Cape Lookout National Seashore at (919) 728-2250 will provide a listing of ferries. Bring walking shoes and some food and drink, as there are no refreshments or transportation available. I made the trip with "Beach Bum Ferry and Guide Service". They also offer Nature and History Tours led by Sonny Williamson, a local author.Their telephone number is (919)729-2331. The cost is $10 or $12 per person, round trip. The guided tour is more expensive. The trip was made interesting by sightings of the wild horses that live on the barrier islands enroute to Core Banks.

**TALES AND LEGENDS.** None now known. The lighthouse is a National Historic Landmark, and as such, has focussed on teaching school children all they want to know about lighthouses. The "School Fund" that supports that activity has been cut, and is in jeopardy of nonrenewal. On-site donations are accepted and appreciated.

So to the night-wandering sailors, pale of fears,
Wide o'er the watery waste a light appears,
Which on the far seen mountains blazing high,
Streams from some lonely watch-tower in the sky.

Homer

14

# BALD HEAD ISLAND LIGHTHOUSE

HISTORY. The state of North Carolina started a lighthouse at Bald Head on Smith Island in 1791 at the mouth of the Cape Fear River, to warn ships of the danger of Frying Pan Shoals, which lay off Cape Fear. Federal funds were appropriated in April, 1792 to complete it, and twice more, so that the light was finally lit in 1796. In 1818, the current tower was built nearby. It was inadequate to guide ships past Frying Pan Shoals, but operated until shut down by the Confederates in 1861. Five years later , a new screw-pile lighthouse was built at Federal  Point and the Bald Head light was discontinued. In 1879 the Federal Point light was also discontinued, and the Bald Head Light Station was reactivated, with a fourth-order lens, marking it as a harbor light. The Cape Fear light, a skelton tower with a first-order lens was built on the far end of Smith Island in 1903. It became obsolete in 1958 and was destroyed. Bald Head remained active until 1935, when it was terminally deactivated. In 1963 the lighthouse was sold to a private owner, who later sold it to the Carolina

Cape Fear Corporation. Subsequently, the Old Baldy Foundation came into being to restore the lighthouse and possibly to create a museum there. A visit in 1995 found the interior of the lighthouse restored, but the exterior was in need of attention.

The tower's light was 110 feet above sea level. 123 steps lead to the top, with the final 10 a ladder.

**MUSEUM.** None on site. A plaque in front of the lighthouse read;

" R. Cochran, Founder

A.D. 1817

D.S. Way, Builder"

**GETTING THERE.** Bald Head Island (now so named) can be reached by ferry from Indigo Plantation in Southport. (Call the ticket office at 910-457-5003 for reservations on the ferry.) The ferry costs $15 round trip, and there is a $4 parking fee. The island is well developed, and special tours, or golf outings can be arranged by calling 910-457-7390. If you wish you may merely take the ferry and walk on the island, or you may rent a bicycle or golf cart by calling Island Wheels at 910-457-4944.

**TALES AND LEGENDS.** None now known.

*The sea thinks for me*
*As I listen and ponder;*
*the sea thinks and every*
*boom of the wave repeats my prayer.*
                              *Richard Jeffries*

# OAK ISLAND LIGHT, CASWELL, N.C.

**HISTORY.** Two lighthouses or beacons were built on Oak Island in 1849 to help navigation on the Cape Fear River. The terms "lighthouse" and "beacon" were used interchangeably in the enabling legislation and are still used so today. They were found to be inadequate, since they were too close to each other.

The present lighthouse was built in 1958, using a Swedish developed moving slip-form technique. Concrete was poured into a form, and when it hardened, the form was moved up to complete another section. This process created a cylindrical tower, not a tapered one, as earlier construction had. The lantern gallery was set in place by helicopter. The color is integrated into the concrete, the top third black, the middle third white, and the bottom third gray.

The tower is 169 ft. tall, with 134 vertical ladder steps to the lantern room. The main light is a four light rotating fixture, using 24 inch parabolic mirrors and 1000 watt quartz bulbs to cast light 24 miles offshore. Its light signature is one flash per second for four seconds, followed by a six second off period.

This is probably the last manually operated lighthouse in the Coast Guard. Duty personnel turn the light on one hour before sunset and turn it off one hour after sunrise, as well as in times of reduced visibility.

The lighthouse is not open to the general public for safety reasons. However, the public is welcome to visit the station and take pictures of the lighthouse.

If duty does not interfer, one may even be given a tour of the station by a Coast Guard guide.

**MUSEUM OR INTERPRETIVE SERVICE.** None, except as mentioned above.

**GETTING THERE.** Exit I-95 at Lumberton. Go east on State Road 211. Pass Supply and Smith, turning south (right) onto S.R. 133 to its end. Turn left onto unmarked road. Coast Guard station is on your left.

**TALES AND LEGENDS.** None now known.

A LIGHTHOUSE POEM, by John D. Carey (Reprinted from THE LIGHTHOUSE DIGEST, by permission)

In times of darkness you provide a light,
Shining through the dark of night,
You guide ships in navigation,
And lead them to their destinations,
Through thick fog and such conditions,
You provide a reassuring vision,
You help them to maintain a course,
And lead them to awaiting shores,
You show them all that you are there,
By shining your bright light through the air,
And through even the most trying times,
We know our way your light will find.

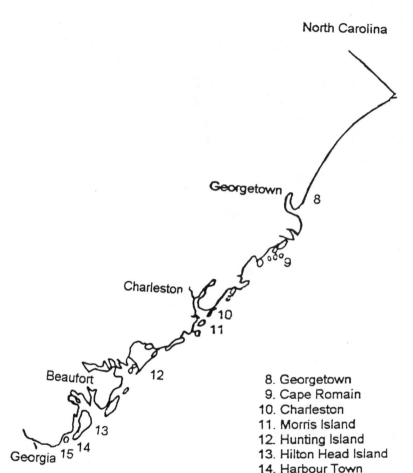

North Carolina

Georgetown 8

9

Charleston

10
11

Beaufort 12

13

Georgia 15 14

8. Georgetown
9. Cape Romain
10. Charleston
11. Morris Island
12. Hunting Island
13. Hilton Head Island
14. Harbour Town
15. Daufuskie Island

**SOUTH CAROLINA**

19

## GEORGETOWN LIGHTHOUSE, S.C.

HISTORY. North Island lies at the entrance to Winyah Bay. Three lighthouses have been built on this island.The first was a wooden tower seventy-two feet high that stood from 1801 until a storm took it in 1806. The next one, of the same height, was built in 1812 of brick painted white. The tower was rebuilt again in 1867, after some damage had been done during the Civil War. This tower is eighty-five feet high, and has 124 steps to the top. The lens are fourth order fresnel. The light signal is 2 flashes separated by a 2 second and a 7 second break.

MUSEUM OR INTERPRETIVE SERVICE. None.

GETTING THERE. From I-95 take Exit 22 east to Georgetown. North Island can only be reached by boat. Launch your own at the Shrine ramp on Boulevard St. or at a launch ramp on South Island Road. Captain Sandy's tours also has a tour boat that will go to North Island. Reservations can by made by calling 803-527-4106. The lighthouse is not open to the public. North Island is now utilized as a youth rehabilitation center by the State of South Carolina.

20

**TALES AND LEGENDS.** Georgetown loves its ghosts! Writer Elizabeth Robertson Huntsinger in her book "Ghosts of Georgetown" writes about twenty ghosts and hauntings. One tale relating to the lighthouse is the sad story of a lighthouse keeper and his small daughter-a cheerful, pretty blond girl. Twice a month they crossed Winyah Bay for supplies, going in and out with the tides. One day as they were heading back to North Island, a storm blew up. It worsened and capsized the rowboat. The keeper tied the little girl onto his back and swam for shore. He made it, but the poor girl had drowned on his back. For many years thereafter, a little girl would appear to seamen to warn them of approaching storms. Those that listened, survived. Those that did not listen often perished.

Shrimpers report a figure who walks the beach with a lighted lantern when the weather turns foul. The old lighthouse keepers once did that.

Yet a third tale was told to me by a young Coast Guardsman, Fireman Alan Cassell. He reported tools missing, things moved, etc. He played a tape for me made in the lighthouse after everyone had left. It recorded sounds much like weary footsteps. He swore that the sounds were not from living feet.

*AN OLD ENGLISH FOLK SONG*

*My father was the keeper of the Eddystone Light,*
*And he slept with a mermaid one fine night.*
*From that union there came three,*
*A porpoise, a porgy, and the other was me.*
*Yo ho ho, the wind blows free;*
*Oh for the life of the rolling sea.*

# CAPE ROMAIN, S.C.

HISTORY. The first of two lighthouses was built at Cape Romain in 1827. It was erected on Raccoon Key, later to be renamed Lighthouse Island and made a part of the Cape Romain National Wildlife Refuge.

The tower at 65 feet was too short, so a new octagonal one, 150 feet tall with 195 steps to the top, was built in 1857. It utilized the lantern room from the first one, and boasted a first order fresnel lens.

The lens and lantern room were destroyed in 1861 by Confederates, but it was repaired and back in service in 1866. There followed a series of cracks and foundation settling, which threw the light out of alignment. The shifting stopped around 1891, and the lighthouse continued to serve until 1947, when it was reduced to a daymark. The stairs in the smaller tower are gone. The site was abandoned in 1960, and the keeper's houses razed. Hurricane Hugo would have destroyed them, anyway.

GOOD NEWS! Both towers have undergone renovation, with a red paint job for the old tower, and a black and white one for alternate faces (the tower is octagonal) on the upper half of the newer tower. The bottom half is all white. The renovation included window sashes and glass.

MUSEUM OR INTERPRETIVE SERVICE. None now available.

**GETTING THERE.** From I-95 take Exit 86 onto I-26 to Charleston. In Charleston pick U.S. 17 north, and follow it about 20 miles to See Wee Road, which leads to the Cape Romain Wildlife Refuge Headquarters. Moores Landing is about five miles in.

Coastal Expeditions is exclusive contractor with the U.S. Fish and Wildlife Service to carry passengers throughout the refuge. You can charter a small boat and captain from them to take you to Lighthouse Island. Call 803- 881-4582 for more information.

**TALES AND LEGENDS.** Fred Wichmann grew up at the lighthouse, where his father, August Frederich Wichmann was the head keeper for 21 years. Fred remembers seeing faint blood stains on the floor of the keeper's cottage. He retells a tale of a Norwegian keeper named Fischer whose wife inherited gold and jewelry from her former husband. She wanted to use some of the money to visit her homeland, but her husband did not want her to go. On a stormy night they had a terrible argument, and she ran from the house to hide her treasure. When she came back the keeper was waiting for her with a butcher knife , and he stabbed her to death. Mrs. Fischer was buried on the island, and was thought a suicide until the keeper confessed to her killing on his own deathbed.

It is reported that her restless spirit roams the island on stormy nights, moaning and crying as she searches for her treasure, never reported found.

--*These blessed candles of the night.*
*William Shakespeare*

23

# SULLIVAN'S ISLAND LIGHT

( Charleston Light)

HISTORY. The main channel in Charleston Harbor shifted, rendering the Morris Island lighthouse useless. A new lighthouse was built in 1962 to serve the area. It was originally painted orange and white, but local residents wanted a more traditional look. The unusual three sided tower was soon repainted black and white.

It is unique in two other ways. The first is that it is the only lighthouse in the nation with an elevator, which is reported to work only sporadically. The second is that the light mechanism is capable of being the most powerful light in the world, with a potential output of 28,000,000 candlepower. Full power is rarely used.

The tower is 163 feet high, and has a range of 26 nautical miles. It was fully automated in 1982. The light shows two flashes every thirty seconds.

MUSEUM OR INTERPRETIVE SERVICE. None readily available. Fort Moultrie, a short distance past the lighthouse, is well worth a visit for history buffs.

GETTING THERE. Drive north on U.S. 17 from Charleston. Take SC 703 through Mt. Pleasant to Sullivan's Island. Follow signs to Fort Moultrie. Look left, and go the short block. The lighthouse is closed.

TALES AND LEGENDS. None now known.

24

# MORRIS ISLAND, S.C.
## (Old Charleston Light)

**HISTORY.** The first lighthouse of record in Charleston Harbor was built in 1767 on Morris Island, which was then a substantial island. It was 102 feet tall. A first order fresnel lens was installed and lit in 1858, but was destroyed, along with the tower, during the Civil War. A new tower was built 400 yards from the old site. This also had a first order lens, and stood 161 feet high. This tower survived an earthquake and hurricanes. It was automated in 1932, and taken out of service in 1962, when the channel shifted. The tower now stands in water, the island having eroded .

**MUSEUM OR INTERPRETIVE SERVICE.** None.

**GETTING THERE.** The lighthouse lies offshore, but is visible from Folly Beach. A boat is needed to reach it. From I-95, take I-26 south to Charleston, turning south onto SC 171 to Folly Island. Turn left onto East Ashley, following it to its end at the gate of the abandoned Coast Guard Station. Walk to the beach, turning left at the beach. You will see the lighthouse in the distance.

**TALES AND LEGENDS.** A Georgia congressman, flying down the coast, spotted the tower and wanted the bricks for a house. He suggested that a Savannah wrecking firm bid to demolish the tower, keeping the bricks. Fred Wichmann, local son of a lighthouse keeper(see Cape Romain) got wind of this and with the aid of the late L. Mendel Rivers stopped the plan. It now belongs to F.E. Felkel, a private developer.

25

# HUNTING ISLAND, S.C.

**HISTORY.** The first lighthouse was built on Hunting Island in 1859. It lasted until around 1862, when it was destroyed, either by erosion or by Confederate forces. A new tower was completed in 1875 about a mile inland from the old site. It was wisely constructed of curved cast-iron sections, each weighing 1200 pounds, that could be dismantled and reassembled when necessary. By 1889 the sea had cut away some of the northern end of the island, so the lighthouse was moved to its current site.

The light had a second order fresnel lens, giving off a bright 100,000 candlepower which could be seen for 18 miles at sea. The tower is 140 feet high, with 181 steps to the top. It is open to the public. Beware of "lighthouse leg". (See glossary). The lighthouse was retired in 1933, and became a part of Hunting Island State Park in 1938.

**MUSEUM OR INTERPRETIVE SERVICE.** There are pictures and narratives in one of the storage buildings. Check out the campground store for great souvenirs.

**GETTING THERE.** Take exit 33 from I-95 to U.S. 17 east. Turn onto U.S. 21 east in Gardens Corner. Stay on U.S. 21 through Beaufort to Hunting Island State Park. There is a modest per car admission fee.

**TALES AND LEGENDS.** None now known.

# HILTON HEAD ISLAND, S.C.

**HISTORY.** A lighthouse was proposed on Hilton Head Island as early as 1854. Two lighthouses were finally built on the island in 1863 with the help of Union troops stationed at Port Royal. The front range light was blown down in 1869. The rear range light operated from 1881 until the 1930's.

The tower is 95 feet high with 112 steps to the top. The lantern, when it shone, was 136 feet above sea level. It is located on private property on a golf course in the Palmetto Dunes Resort. The tower was restored in 1985-6.

**MUSEUM.** None known.

**GETTING THERE.** See the instructions for reaching Hilton Head Island in unit on Harbour Town. Permission to visit it might be obtained by contacting the Director of Public Relations, Greenwood Development Corp. at 803/785-1106.

**TALES AND LEGENDS.** The August 1898 hurricane was expected. The Weather Bureau had given ample warning. Keeper Adam Fripp and his twenty-two year old daughter, Caroline, laid in supplies and waited.

The rain started on Saturday morning and continued all day. Adam stayed in the lighthouse, and sent Caroline to secure the house. She took sandwiches to her father during a lull in the rain, and noticed that his face had the greyish tinge it had taken on after his mild heart attack the year before.

The storm was getting worse by the minute. Adam had lit the lamp when the gale blew out two of the windows in the lantern room. At two minutes to six the light went out. After several relightings, her father collapsed on the floor with another heart attack. Caroline relit the lamp several times, but she could not keep it lit in such a gale.

Caroline and her father were trapped in the lighthouse by the rising water, which reached levels of four feet deep and more on the island. When the storm passed Caroline half-carried her father through the receding water to their house, where he died in his bed. She never recovered from her sorrow and followed him in death a few weeks later.

Many years have passed, but now and then on stormy nights a girl in a torn and bedraggled blue dress is seen in the lighthouse windows or at the foot of it, or sometimes in or near the keepers cottages. The cottages have been moved to Harbour Town to be used as a retail store. The girl walks in the storm, her dress blown by the wind, weeping and wringing her hands. Thus the "Blue Lady Of Hilton Head".

( Story adapted from "South Carolina Ghosts From the Coast to the Mountains", by Nancy Roberts. Univ. Of South Carolina Press, 1983)

# HARBOUR TOWN, S.C  (Hilton Head Island)

**HISTORY.** This 93 foot hexagonal tower, built in 1969, was the first one built with private funds since 1817. It is the symbol of the Sea Pines Plantation. It is included in this book because it is so familiar to golf fans and visitors to the island. The light, which flashes every 2.5 seconds faces Calibogue Sound and is an aid to inland waterway travelers. It is not recognized as an official U. S lighthouse. It is open to the public daily from 8:00 am until dark. 110 steps lead to the top.

**MUSEUM OR INTERPRETIVE SERVICE.** None.

**GETTING THERE.** From I-95 southbound, take exit 28 following SC 462 to US 278. Northbound take US 321 south to SC 170 north to US 278, south. Go to Sea Pines Circle. Get onto Greenwood Drive. There is a small entry fee per car. Follow Lighthouse Road to Harbour Town. The area surrounding the lighthouse is a diverse shopping and eating area as well as a marina containing many fine boats.

**TALES AND LEGENDS.** The only tale now known relates to sounds and sights of a ghost in the buildings that were once the keeper's cottages at the Old Hilton Head Island lighthouse. This was written up in a 1984 edition of "The Hilton Head Islander", and is detailed in the Hilton Head Island Lighthouse section.

# DAUFUSKIE ISLAND, S.C.

**HISTORY.** Daufuskie Island is just across Calibogue Sound from Hilton Head Island. Early records refer to it as "Mongin Island", named after Captain John Mongin who claimed he was granted the island by King George II in 1740. Two sets of navigational lights were constructed on the island. One set, the Haig Point range lights, (also referred to as the Daufuskie Island Lights), served from October, 1873 to July, 1924. The rear beacon, mounted on the keeper's house, had a fifth order fresnel lens. The second set, built on Bloody Point, served from 1883 to 1922. The rear light of this set was also mounted on top of the keeper's house. Both houses are still standing. The Haig Point house serves as a bed and breakfast for members of the Haig Point Resort Community. The light has been removed from the Bloody Point house.

**MUSEUM OR INTERPRETIVE SERVICE.** None known. Ex Postmistress Mrs. Billie Burn, a direct descendant of Arthur Burn, (see tale below) provided much of the information in this section, as well as the great picture on the next page.

**GETTING THERE.** The island can be reached by private boat, launching at Alljoy Landing near Bluffton. There is a public dock on the island, but no public transportation. Arrange beforehand or walk or bike. Vagabond Cruises run a tour boat from Hilton Head Island. Call (803) 842-4155 for times and rates.

**TALES AND LEGENDS.** During the Yemassee Indian War of 1715, island settlers trapped and massacred a group of Indians on the southeastern tip of the island. One survived and swam to Tybee Island. Hence the name,"Bloody Point". The word "Daufuskie" translates to "place of blood".

Twelve year old Nick Beatty's family had moved into the old Haig Point keepers house. Nick had visits from an old man he knew as Arthur, who told him stories of the island. No one else ever saw Arthur, but the old rocking chair in the Beatty living room was seen to rock now and then.

Arthur Burn was the last keeper of the light. After his retirement, he became ill and was taken to the mainland for care. When he returned he swore he would never leave his house and his island again. The words he used were" I'm going to stay in this house forever!" Did he ? ( This tale was printed in "South Carolina Ghosts From the Coast to the Mountains", by Nancy Roberts.)

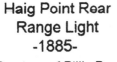

Haig Point Rear
Range Light
-1885-
Courtesy of Billie Burn

31

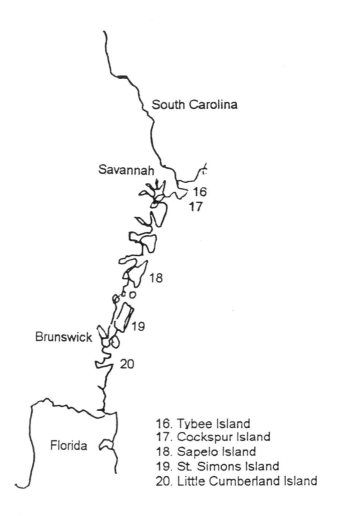

South Carolina

Savannah

16
17

18

19

Brunswick

20

Florida

16. Tybee Island
17. Cockspur Island
18. Sapelo Island
19. St. Simons Island
20. Little Cumberland Island

**GEORGIA**

# COCKSPUR ISLAND, GA.

**HISTORY.** In 1848 two small lighthouses were constructed in the Savannah River to guide ships past Tybee Island and around Elba and Cockspur Islands. One of them, the "North Channel Light" did not survive the Civil War. The other, alternately called the South Channel light, and the Cockspur Island Light, did. It was relit after the Civil War and served continuously until 1909. It was then used as a harbor beacon, and was finally retired  in 1949. It fell into disrepair, and was transferred to the National Park Service in 1956. It was restored in 1979. It is not operating, but is open to the public.

**MUSEUM OR INTERPRETIVE SERVICE.** None on site, but perspective can be gotten from a visit to Fort Pulaski National Monument and to the Tybee Island Lighthouse and museum a few miles ahead on Tybee Island.

**GETTING THERE.** See Instructions for Tybee Island Lighthouse. Cockspur is on the way to Tybee. It is offshore. Those who seek adventure can swim or wade to the lighthouse. My son Eric and I did. Wiser minds recommend going by boat. We second that, since the tide turned on us, and we had to wade through swamp up to Fort Pulaski. A messy business!

**TALES AND LEGENDS.** George W. Martus served as keeper of the Cockspur Island Light. He lived on Elba Island with his sister, Florence. One day Florence went to Fort Pulaski to spend the afternoon with her father, who had fought there. Several sailors, whose ship was docked in Savannah, also visited the Fort that day. Her father offered to show them the island, and tell them tales of the battle. While he was doing so, Florence caught the eye of one of the sailors. He asked if he could call on her , and did so several times while his ship was in port. Before he left, he promised to return and marry her. ( Have other sailors used that line?)

"I'll wait for you always", she told him. As his ship pulled away, Florence stood in front of her cottage waving a white handkerchief.

The sailor never returned. For more than fifty years, Florence Martus waved in vain at every passing ship, hoping her love would return. She did, however, win the hearts of sailors, and of the city of Savannah. There is a statue of her on River Street in Savannah, standing next to a faithful dog, waving a handkerchief. Many sailors brought her gifts from abroad, including a llama from Peru, but Florence remained true to her one love throughout her life. She now lives in history as the "Waving Girl" of Savannah.

" For the lighthouse had become almost invisible, had melted away into the blue haze."

Virginia Woolf

# TYBEE ISLAND, GA.

**HISTORY.** The phrase "From Tybee Light to Rabun Gap" has often been used to describe the State of Georgia. One of the first public structures built under General James Oglethorpe in the new colony of Georgia was a beacon on Tybee Island. The tower was completed by William Blytheman in 1736. The octagonal daymark was 90 feet tall, with a base of 25 feet. Three new towers were built, in 1740, 1757 and 1773. The last of these was lit with spermaceti candles in 1790.

A second order fresnel lens was installed in 1857. The lighthouse grounds were occupied by Union soldiers during the Civil War. Nonetheless, a keg of dynamite was exploded in the tower by The Irish Jasper Greens in 1862, rendering the lighthouse useless. It was rebuilt in 1867 with a first order fresnel lens. The first electric lamp was turned on in the lighthouse in 1933. It currently has a 750 watt white light of 30,000 candlepower, visible at night for 20 miles at sea. The light is constant.

The tower is 154 feet high, with 178 steps to the top. The octagonal brick tower has had several designs over the years. It was initially all white, followed in 1890 with a white top and black bottom. In 1920 it was painted with black-white-black wide stripes. The current paint job, black top and white bottom, was applied in 1970.

**MUSEUM OR INTERPRETIVE SERVICE.** The entire lighthouse grounds are a museum, with the oil house and the keeper's cottage fully restored. Restoration is continuing. One small house has a great video, and the gift shop offers a variety of lighthouse related gifts and materials to tempt anyone. The museum and lighthouse are open to visitors daily except Tuesdays from 10:00 am to 6:00 pm. Admission to both is $3.00 for adults, $1 for ages 6-12, and $2.00 for seniors.

The Tybee Island Historical Society, P.O. Box 366, Tybee Island, Ga. 31328 offers memberships to interested wickies, including free admission to the museum and lighthouse, as well as a discount on purchases and a newsletter.

Across the street from the lighthouse museum is another museum in what was once Fort Screven. It is a storehouse of artifacts and memorabilia from Tybee from the seventeenth century through the Second World War. There is a small admission fee.

**GETTING THERE.** From I-95 take Ga. 204 east into Savannah. Turn right(east) onto Victory Drive (Ga. 26) to Tybee Island. When you reach the island a sign on your left will direct you to the lighthouse. Take note of Fort Pulaski and a fine view of the Cockspur Island lighthouse as you drive the road to Tybee Island.

**TALES AND LEGENDS.** During the Civil War, Union troops occupied the lighthouse grounds on Tybee. They had been shelling Fort Pulaski, to little avail, until the Union artillery received rifled cannon. Rifled shells were fired into the powder magazine wall, threatening a breach. The Commandant was forced to surrender. This presaged the end of such walled forts.

# SAPELO ISLAND, GA.

**HISTORY.** The Sapelo Island lighthouse was built byCaptain Winslow Lewis in 1820, installing a 15 inch reflector-type light. A fourth order fresnel lens was added in 1854. The light was damaged during the Civil War, but was repaired and put back into service in 1868.The first lighthouse was lost to erosion, and a tower 65 feet tall, with black and white stripes, was built in 1877. The foundation was undermined by a hurricane in 1898. It was replaced in 1905 by a 100 foot high steel tower which served until it was deactivated in 1933. The lighthouse is currently  (1998) undergoing complete restoration. The cistern and oil house will also be restored.

**MUSEUM OR INTERPRETIVE SERVICE.** A fine museum and gift shop are in the Visitor's Center.

**GETTING THERE.** Sapelo Island can only be visited if prior permission is obtained.(call 912-485-2299 or FAX 485-2140), or a day tour can be arranged through the Sapelo Island Visitor's Center (912-437-3224). The dock is on Ga. 99 east of I-95.

**TALES AND LEGENDS.** None now known.

# ST. SIMONS LIGHTHOUSE, GA.

**HISTORY.** James Gould built the first St. Simons Lighthouse in 1808 near the site of the present structure. He was also the first lighthouse keeper, serving until his retirement in 1837. The tower was 75 feet tall, built of tabby and brick, and topped by an iron lantern ten feet tall. A third order fresnel lens was installed in 1857, marking the lighthouse as a true coastal light.

During the Civil War, the island was held by the Macon Artillery with six field guns stationed at Fort Brown, just west of the lighthouse. In 1862 the fort was abandoned and Gould's lighthouse was destroyed. ( The story of James Gould and his trials on St. Simons was told by Eugenia Price in her book "Lighthouse" ,1971.)

A tower of 110 feet with 129 cast iron steps was built near the old site in 1872. It was designed by Charles Cluskey. The lighthouse was modified and updated in 1877. The third order fresnel lens were aided by electrification in 1934. The lighthouse was fully automated in 1954. Its 1,000 watt mogul electric lamp shines nightly, and is visible for 18 miles.

A National Park Service historic preservation team has recently rehabilitated the lighthouse, repainting it both inside and outside.

**MUSEUM OR INTERPRETIVE SERVICE.**The Museum of Coastal History occupies the Keeper's Quarters. It houses a gift shop, and several rooms have been decorated and furnished in 1800's decor. The lighthouse is open for climbing, and memberships are available in the Coastal Georgia History Society, P.O. Box 21136, St. Simons Island, Ga. 31522. Hours of operation are 10:00 a.m. to 5:00 p.m. Monday through Saturday. Sunday hours are 1:30 p.m. to 5:00 p.m. A small fee is required for admission to the museum and lighthouse.

**GETTING THERE.** Take Exit 10 from I-95, head east to U.S. 17, south. Turn east at the St. Simons Island signs, paying a small toll to get onto the island. Once there, follow Ocean Boulevard to The Village. the lighthouse and museum are one block further.

**TALES AND LEGENDS.** A dispute between the head keeper, Mr. Fred Osborne and his assistant boiled over one morning in March, 1880. In the duel that was fought, Osborne was killed. His footsteps have been reported on the tower steps, especially in foul weather. The footsteps have been especially noticed by the wives of keepers who, upon hearing them, and presuming them to be those of their husbands, have heated a planned meal, only to have the meal grow cold as the expected keeper did not appear.

If you catch a glimpse of a young woman walking the beaches, lantern in hand, it will probably be Mary the Wanderer, still searching for the lover who was drowned when his boat capsized off St. Simons Beach, 100 years or so ago.

# LITTLE CUMBERLAND ISLAND, GA.

**HISTORY.** The need for a lighthouse on St. Andrew's Sound was felt early. John Hastings of Boston built the tower in 1838, with a focal plane of 78 feet above mean high tide and a third order fresnel lens.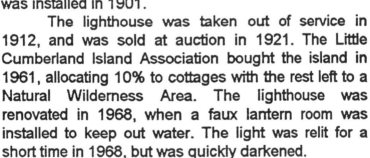
The lighthouse was slightly damaged during the Civil War ,and was alternately manned by both sides. Encroachment occurred by 1876, so a brick wall was built around the tower, filled with concrete and bricked over. A new iron deck was installed in 1901.

The lighthouse was taken out of service in 1912, and was sold at auction in 1921. The Little Cumberland Island Association bought the island in 1961, allocating 10% to cottages with the rest left to a Natural Wilderness Area. The lighthouse was renovated in 1968, when a faux lantern room was installed to keep out water. The light was relit for a short time in 1968, but was quickly darkened.

Architect Walter Sedovic of Locust Valley, N.Y. supervised another restoration effort in 1994-95.

**GETTING THERE.** This is a privately owned and protected island. Captain Reynolds (912-265-0392) at the Jekyll Island Marina will take a charter by the lighthouse for viewing and photographing.

**TALES AND LEGENDS.** None now known.

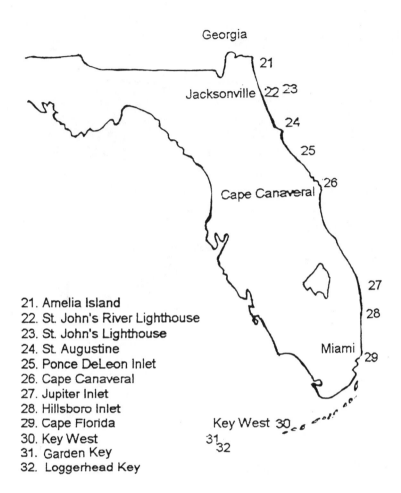

Georgia

21

Jacksonville 22 23

24

25

26

Cape Canaveral

27

28

21. Amelia Island
22. St. John's River Lighthouse
23. St. John's Lighthouse
24. St. Augustine
25. Ponce DeLeon Inlet
26. Cape Canaveral
27. Jupiter Inlet
28. Hillsboro Inlet
29. Cape Florida
30. Key West
31. Garden Key
32. Loggerhead Key

Miami
29

Key West 30

31
32

# FLORIDA-EAST COAST

# AMELIA ISLAND, FLA.

**HISTORY.** In 1820 a lighthouse was built on Cumberland Island. It was dismantled and moved to Amelia Island in 1836, where it could serve the St. Marys river traffic better. The tapered tower sits on a promontory, showing a light 107 feet above sea level, in spite of its 64 feet of height.

The third order fresnel lens were made by Barbier Bernard of France and installed after the 1852 report on lighthouses.

The lantern rotated on a ball race which was turned by a clock drum that had to be rewound every four hours. The light has been electrified and automated. The light signal is a 2.5 second flash, with sectional red covering the shoal water in Nassau Sound, and white for the remainder. The white can be seen for 23 miles, the red for 19.

**MUSEUM OR INTERPRETIVE SERVICE.** None.

**GETTING THERE.** From I-95 take Exit 129 onto A1A east to Amelia Island. In Fernandina turn left onto Wolff St. ,left onto Lighthouse Circle and Lane.

**TALES AND LEGENDS.** The small size of the lighthouse did not allow an assistant to the keeper. In 1881 the keeper injured one of his big toes, and his wife had to carry on his duties until he recovered the use of his foot. Such was the case in smaller facilities.

42

# ST. JOHNS RIVER LIGHT STATION, FLA.

**HISTORY.** The first lighthouse in this area was built in 1830 at a cost of $10,550.00. It was undermined by encroachment, and another was built in 1835. Further efforts to secure the lighthouse were minimal, since title to the site had not been obtained. Title finally was obtained in 1857, and a new tower was built across the bar in 1859. A Confederate sympathizer shot out the light in the early 1860's. The lighthouse was rebuilt in 1867, and was raised 15 feet in 1887 to a height of 81 feet, with a third order fresnel lens. There followed a storm of complaints from shipping interests, claiming that the lighthouse was inadequate for the job. A 150-foot lighthouse was proposed for St. George Island, but was never built.

The light was discontinued in 1929, when a radio beacon was installed on the St. Johns Lightship. In 1969 the Navy bought 350 surrounding acres for the Mayport Naval Station. The red brick tower was placed on the Historic Register in 1982, and in 1983 was restored. It is accessible, but is unattended.

**MUSEUM OR INTERPRETIVE SERVICE.** None.

**GETTING THERE.** The lighthouse is on the Mayport Naval Station. From !-95 take Fla. 105 east to the Mayport ferry. In Mayport follow the signs to the base. Show your driver's license, registration and insurance.

**TALES AND LEGENDS.** None now known.

43

# ST. JOHNS LIGHT STATION

**HISTORY.** The St. Johns River was an important port. When the old lighthouse was found to be lacking, the lightship Brunswick was moved from Brunswick, Ga. and renamed the St. Johns Lightship. It served from 1929 until 1954, when a non-traditional lighthouse was built adjoining a building on the Mayport Naval base that currently houses a Coast Guard contingent.

The 64-foot concrete lighthouse boasts a single aero-marine beacon of 200,000 candlepower which can be seen 22 nautical miles at sea. It has been completely automated since 1967, with a built-in alarm system that alerts the Coast Guard of a malfunction. This lighthouse resembles the automated light on Egmont Key near St. Petersburg.

While the modern shape may disappoint the lighthouse afficiando, it does not disappoint the mariner, who appreciates the brightness nonetheless.

**MUSEUM OR INTERPRETIVE SERVICE.** None.

**GETTING THERE.** See St. Johns River Light. Once on Mayport Naval Base, go north on Maine St., east on Moale Ave., and one block north on Baltimore St.

**TALES AND LEGENDS.** None now known.

44

# ST. AUGUSTINE, FLA.

HISTORY. The first lighthouse in the Florida territory was at St. Augustine. A coquina-stone tower that had been built by the Spanish as a part of a chapel was strengthened and rebuilt to support an iron lantern. It displayed a fixed white light generated by 10 Winslow Lewis patented Argand lamps with 14 inch reflectors. It was lit on April 4, 1824.

In 1855 a harbor light with a fourth order fresnel lens was built. It was destroyed during the civil war, and rebuilt in 1867. Beach erosion caused a new tower to be built about a half mile from the old site. Finished in 1874, the light has a focal plane height of 161 feet, and the first order fresnel lens make it visible for eighteen miles at sea. The tower is 165 feet tall, with 219 steps to the top.

The spiral black and white bands are similar to those of the Cape Hatteras lighthouse, but the red lantern room differentiates the two as day marks.

The light was electrified in 1936, and automated in 1955. It is still an active lighthouse.

MUSEUM OR INTERPRETIVE SERVICE. There is a wonderful museum in the restored keeper's house, the result of a 14 year campaign by the Junior Service League of St. Augustine to restore the house and lighthouse to their Victorian splendor. Artifacts, pictures and memorabilia make this a must stop, as well as a fine video. The gift shop is not to be missed. There are truly wicky "budget busters" to be found there. There is a small admission to both the museum and the lighthouse, $3.50 for both for adults at this writing, and less for seniors and children. Open daily, with extended summer hours.

**GETTING THERE.** From I-95.take Fla. 16 to U.S.1. Turn south to Fla 312, turn east to US A1A,left to Old Beach Road and lighthouse complex.

**TALES AND LEGENDS.** A young Daniels family son was experimenting with parachutes. His unfortunate victim was the black family cat. He first tried the rig from the oil house, and when it worked, threw the cat from the lighthouse. The parachute worked well, but the cat was so frightened it disappeared for several weeks. Returning, it never again approached a child or the lighthouse, and its descendents still do the same.

During the 1930's a seaman lost his billet while his ship was tied up near the lighthouse. He hung himself in a fit of depression in the keeper's house. A young worker doing restoration work in the 1980's reported seeing a man hanging in one of the rooms, but no one could later be found there.

Finally, the staff at the museum report that there is a friendly ghost they have named Albert whose presence has been felt in the basement of the keeper's house. He has not been seen, but has moved things, has made sounds, and has been sensed.

Another interesting sidelight concerning the lighthouse keepers. They were not paid well, and would supplement their income in numerous ways. Keepers might work at other jobs, or sold produce, livestock, and handcrafted items.

46

# PONCE DeLEON INLET, FLA.

**HISTORY.** In order to fill the 95 mile gap between the Cape Canaveral and St. Augustine lighthouses, a new tower was built at Mosquito Inlet in 1835. The inlet was renamed Ponce DeLeon Inlet in 1927, when the name of the erstwhile bug became unpopular with the Chamber of Commerce.(i.e. Mosquito River to Halifax River, Mosquito County to Orange County.) Failure to receive any oil kept the light dark, and in the same year storm waves undermined the tower. The fighting of the Seminole War kept engineers from repairing the damage, and the tower later collapsed.

The current red brick tower was built in Baltimore in 1887, and shipped south. All building supplies had to be lightered ashore, with the loss of at least one life in the process.

The tower is 175 feet tall, with 203 spiraling steps. The light, with a third order fresnel lens, was visible for 19 miles.

The lighthouse was decommissioned in 1970, to be replaced by a beacon mounted on top of the New Smyrna Coast Guard Station. However, the lighthouse was reinstated in 1983 when a sprouting condominium development at New Smyrna Beach obscured the light on top of the Coast Guard building . The old lens are stored in Old Mystic Seaport, in Mystic, Connecticut. The current lantern is a 40,000 candlepower rotating lantern, which has a range of 17 miles.

47

**MUSEUM OR INTERPRETIVE SERVICE.** The Ponce DeLeon Inlet Lighthouse Preservation Association now controls and maintains the grounds and buildings in the complex. There is a well stocked gift shop, and several restored keepers buildings, with period furniture and fixtures. A new building houses the Cape Canaveral first order fresnel lens and several other lens, and the lighthouse is open for climbing, weather permitting. The original catwalk has been replaced for added safety. There is also a restored tugboat, the F.D. Russell on display. Admission is $4.00 for adults and $1.00 for children. Even if you can't visit, become an associate member by sending $7.50 to :Ponce DeLeon Inlet Lighthouse Preservation Association, Inc., 4931 South Peninsula Drive, Ponce Inlet, Fla. 32127. You will receive a membership card and newsletters as well as other benefits.

**GETTING THERE.** From I-95 take U.S. 92 east to South Atlantic Ave, (U.S. A1A). Follow it south (right) to its end, turning left onto Peninsula Ave.

**TALES AND LEGENDS.** The soap opera "As the World Turns" filmed a sequence in the lighthouse, with a man and a woman struggling on the catwalk, with appropriate screaming. The police received three calls reporting trouble in the lighthouse.

A local fisherman fell from his boat, and it drifted away. He swam toward the light, claiming that the lighthouse had saved his life. Not the first!!

Joe Davis, First Assistant Keeper, died of a heart attack in 1919 while climbing the tower. He has been heard in the tower as recently as 1994.

Finally, there have been black and white cats at this lighthouse complex for the past 109 years.

# CAPE CANAVERAL, FLA.

HISTORY. Early Spanish explorers called the hook of sand that juts out into the Atlantic Ocean midway down the east coast of the Florida peninsula *Canaberal* or *Canaveral* which means "place of reeds" or "place of cane", possibly referring to the reed arrows the Ais Indians used to drive off the Spanish.

The first lighthouse on this site was built by local builders who had little knowledge of lighthouses. It was a mere 60 feet tall and actually endangered ships that sailed close enough to shore to see it. Seamen complained loudly.

A 145-foot iron tower was started just prior to the Civil War, but was not completed until 1868, after hostilities. It had a first order fresnel lens and could be seen for 18 nautical miles. In 1873, the tower was painted with black and white horizontal bands similar to those on North Carolina's Bodie Island lighthouse.

The sea moved toward the lighthouse, eventually causing it to be moved. The conical tower, constructed of cast iron lined with bricks, was moved 1 1/2 miles inland in 1884, where it still stands.

The Coast Guard has completed a renovation of the inside and outside of the lighthouse to the tune of $300,000.00. The lighthouse is currently operative.

MUSEUM OR INTERPRETIVE SERVICE. None.

**GETTING THERE.** The lighthouse is on a protected Air Force Base, Cape Canaveral Air Station. Access is controlled. Access is possible through the Coast Guard at (407) 868-4296, but they are overwhelmed. Take SR 528 (Beeline Expressway) east from I-95 to the Bennett Causeway, and follow Cape Canaveral Air Station signs.

**TALES AND LEGENDS.** Captain Mills Burnham held the post of lighthouse keeper from 1853 to 1886. During that time he and his family lived a somewhat isolated existence. One indication of the isolation was the fact that at least three of his five daughters married assistant keepers, probably because they were the only dependable young men available. During the Civil War, Captain Burnham dutifully carried out Confederate Secretary of the Navy Stephen Mallory's order to shut down the lighthouse. He buried the lamps and clockwork in his orange grove near the Banana River, retrieving them after the war, when they were reinstalled in the tower. During the war, Captain Burnham and his family remained on site, raising their own vegetables, catching fish and hunting game.

When Captain Burnham died in 1868, he was buried in his beloved orange grove. He typified the self-reliant, trustworthy people who manned many of America's lighthouses.

*As to the eye of the mariner....*
*appears the light of a fire burning*
*at a solitary spot on the summit of a mountain.*

*Homer*

# JUPITER INLET, FLA.

HISTORY. Designed by Lt. George G. Meade, this lighthouse was built under the most difficult of conditions. Jupiter Inlet became silted shut in 1854. This forced the builders to carry 500 tons of material up the Indian River in shallow draft scows. This, along with mosquitoes, heat and the Third Seminole War caused long delays in the building. The light was finally lit in 1860, only to be extinguished in 1861 when Southern sympathizers, aided by an assistant keeper, hid the lens and lamp. Federal authorities sent Captain James A. Armour to find and bring them to Key West for safe keeping. He returned the lens and lamp after the war, and served as a fine head keeper for over forty years.

The lighthouse was relit in 1866 after the war ended.

The 105-foot tower was a natural brick color for fifty years, but when it became discolored due to internal dampness, it was painted with red art cement sometime around 1910. In 1928, the old system of weights and mineral oil lamps was replaced by rotating electric lamps. In that same year a hurricane broke one of the bullseyes. The pieces were collected and sent to Charleston to be reassembled and to be held together with a brass band. The lighthouse was repainted for its centenary, and the inside was painted within the past decade. The tower stands on a hill, so that the light is 146 feet above sea level, and it can be seen for 25 nautical miles. The Coast Guard maintains the light, which is automated and fully operative.

**MUSEUM OR INTERPRETIVE SERVICE.** There is a delightful gift shop and museum, with a video on the history of the Jupiter Inlet lighthouse to be enjoyed. The lighthouse is open for climbing ( for people over 48 inches tall ). The cost is $5.00 for a guided tour of the lighthouse. At this writing, the gift shop, museum and lighthouse are open from 10:00 to 4:00 Sunday through Wednesday. For information, call (407) 747-8380.The gift shop opened in 1994. Most of the workers are volunteers.

**GETTING THERE.** Jupiter Inlet lighthouse is easily seen from U.S.1. Take the Exit 59 from I-95, turn left onto U.S. 1. Turn right onto Jupiter Drive, and turn right into Burt Reynolds Park.

**TALES AND LEGENDS.** This lighthouse has many tales to tell. In 1872 a Mallory steamer, the Victor, ran aground south of the inlet. The keeper and asistant keeper helped bring the passengers and crew safely ashore. Three dogs, Vic, Storm and Wreck became a part of the lighthouse entourage from this incident.

Pirate treasure, said to be looted from a Mexican church, was reputed to be buried on site. One of the assistant keepers spent much of his free time digging for it. Some pranksters buried an iron pot in the hole. The poor man got so excited when his shovel hit metal, and the disappointment was so great, that he never dug in the hole again, but simply gave up.

During the 1928 hurricane, Captain Seabrook, despite an infected hand, installed the mineral lamps back when the generator was disabled. His sixteen year old son climbed the tower and turned the light manually for four hours, while the tower swayed as much as seventeen inches. What dedication!

52

# HILLSBORO INLET, FLA.

**HISTORY.** The northern limit of the Florida Reef is off the coast of Pompano Beach. Beginning in 1885, the Lighthouse Board annually requested a lighthouse "at or near Hillsboro Point, Florida,...". Finally, action was taken. A lighthouse that had been built for the 1904 Great St. Louis Exposition was bought and a second order fresnel lens installed. The lamps were lit in 1907.

The early fuel was kerosene, which had to be carried up the 175 steps to the lantern room. The light mechanism, as in many early lighthouses, rotated on a mercury filled reservoir, which was later to cause problems. A weight ran down to the watch room. A hand drum which provided the power for rotation had to be rewound every half hour, giving keepers little time to rest while the light was operating.

The spidery structure, with a cylindrical stairway in the middle was a design that allowed wind and waves to pass through without harming the tower.The bottom third is white, to show up against the trees, and the top is black, to show up against the sky.

The light was converted to electricity in the late 1920's, and was upgraded in 1966 to 2,000,000 candlepower. In the 1990's the lighthouse was found to be contaminated by mercury, and was closed to human access. The Coast Guard was limited to attaching a light to the catwalk railing, which carried only an estimated 11 miles. (The original light had a nominal range of 28 miles.) The tower is now clear and the temporary light will be replaced by a vega lantern.

**MUSEUM OR INTERPRETIVE SERVICE.** None.

**GETTING THERE.** Take exit 37 off I-95, or the Deerfield exit off the Florida Turnpike. Go to U.S.A1A, turning south and follow to Lighthouse Point, which is just north of Hillsboro Inlet. The lighthouse is through private property with a guarded gate. Permission may be obtained by calling the Aids to Navigation Officer at Coast Guard Seventh District Headquarters. The phone number is (305) 535-4311. Another alternative is to photograph the lighthouse across the inlet from Pompano Beach. A telephoto lens is helpful. We parked on N.E. 16th St. in a public parking area, and walked along the beach to the inlet.

**TALES AND LEGENDS.** There is a plaque on the lighthouse reservation commemorating the death of the famous "Barefoot Mailman", James E. Hamilton. On October 11, 1887 he found his skiff missing when he came to Hillsboro Inlet. He attempted to swim the inlet, and lost his life in the attempt.

A series of unexplained fires broke out in the area surrounding the lighthouse soon after its lighting. An exhaustive investigation determined that the fires had been caused by the magnifying and concentrating power of the curved diamond panes in the lens.That is why many lighthouses had shades drawn during daylight hours in order to protect the light mechanism from the effects of direct sun, as well as the surrounding area from the magnifying effects of the lens on the sun's rays, and the resulting fires that such exposure could cause. The lens have been removed, since the vega lantern does not need it for magnification. It will be placed in an offshore light.

# CAPE FLORIDA, FLA. ( KEY BISCAYNE)

**HISTORY.** The Florida coast has been claiming ships since the discovery of the area by John Cabot in 1497. Soon after Florida became a territory, the U.S. Government began extending the string of lighthouses it had been building along the Atlantic coast. Samuel B. Lincoln built a 65 foot tower of brick, tapering it from five feet at the base to two feet at the top, completing it in 1825. It was discovered, several years later, that the builder had cheated in the construction, making the walls hollow instead of solid, as was stated in his contract. No one was ever prosecuted for this omission.

The lighthouse was partially destroyed in an Indian attack in 1836 (see below) and was finally repaired in 1846. It was not an adequate light, however, and in 1855 was raised to 95 feet and a fresnel lens ( probably third order) was installed.

Once again, in 1861, the lighthouse was put out of commission, this time by Confederate raiders. It was relit in 1867.

The light was taken out of service in 1878, when the Fowey Rock light, (located two miles southeast of Key Biscayne) was lit. The historic lighthouse was not finished, however. One hundred years later, on July 4, 1978, the light was again relit.

55

**MUSEUM OR INTERPRETIVE SERVICE.** This is one of our lucky lighthouses. On July 27, 1996, a celebration was held to commemorate the restoration of the outside and inside of the lighthouse. (Time and weather, especially hurricanes, had taken a toll of the outside bricks.) Restoration of the keeper's cottage and kitchen are currently underway. When all is reopened, you will be able to climb the 121 steps to the top and perhaps see a recreation of a Seminole siege. ( Call (305) 361-8779 for information.)

**GETTING THERE.** From I-95 take the exit marked 25th Rd., following signs to the Rickenbacker Causeway. Cross the causeway ($1.00 toll) and stay on Crandon Blvd. to its end, which will be the entrance to Bill Baggs Cape Florida State Recreation Area. Admission is $4.00 per car, or $2.00 for driver only.

**TALES AND LEGENDS.** On July 23, 1836, during the Second Seminole War, a Seminole war party attacked the lighthouse. The Assistant Keeper, John Thompson and a helper named Henry fled to the tower, reaching it just in time. The Indians set fire to the door, which in turn ignited a 225 gallon oil tank. The two men ran up the lighthouse with a keg of gunpowder, bullets and a musket. The fire soon drove them onto the open platform, exposing them to gunfire from below. Henry was killed and a wounded Thompson lay still.The attackers, thinking him dead, left the lighthouse,and plundered and set fire to the quarters.

The explosion was heard by a U.S. Navy ship, the U.S.S. Concord. The next afternoon sailors in two ship's boats came ashore and rescued Thompson. He was treated at Key West and taken to Charleston, S.C. where he fully recuperated.

# KEY WEST, FLA.

**HISTORY.** The first lighthouse on Key West was built on Whitehead Point in 1825. Fourteen refuge seekers were swept away by a hurricane in 1846, along with the lighthouse in which they had sought shelter.

A 65 foot tower was built on a rise away from the beach in 1847, and was raised to 85 feet in 1894, in response to complaints from mariners. The lighthouse is 100 feet above mean high tide. It has a second order fresnel lens that magnifies a 175 watt halide light, with three red sector panels identifying shoal waters.

The lighthouse was taken out of service in 1969. It was restored to its 1847 appearance, repainted white and placed back into service in 1989, its light automatically turning on at dusk.

**MUSEUM OR INTERPRETIVE SERVICE.** There is a great museum, with models, pictures, artifacts, seven fresnel lenses, a gift shop, and a sweeping view of the island after an 88 step climb to the lighthouse balcony. Hours are 9:30 to 4:30 daily except Christmas. Admission is $5 for adults, $1 for children.

**GETTING THERE.** In Key West, southwest on North Roosevelt Blvd. to Truman Ave. to 938 Whitehead St.

**TALES AND LEGENDS.** None now known.

# GARDEN KEY, FLA. (Fort Jefferson)

**HISTORY.** Ponce de Leon first discovered the seven rocky islets that lie 70 miles west of Key West in 1513, and called them Las Tortugas (the turtles) because of the many turtles there, some of which replenished his party's dwindling food supply. They later were called the Dry Tortugas in light of the hot,dry conditions.

In 1821 the Navy drove out the pirates that had claimed the area, and began consideration of a lighthouse on one of the islands. They chose Bush Key, later to be renamed Garden Key, and built the first lighthouse there in 1825. The tower was 75 feet tall, and it served quietly until 1846, when the Army began building Fort Jefferson, the largest masonry fort the U.S. had ever built, but never completed. The Army abandoned the fort in 1874 after 40,000 bricks had been laid. The guns of the fort, however, were never fired in battle.

The islands went through a period of abandonement until 1935, when President Franklin D. Roosevelt declared seven of the islands, including Garden Key, a national monument.

In 1858 the Lighthouse Board created a new light on Loggerhead Key (see next entry) , placing the first order fresnel lens in the new light, and reducing the one on Garden Key to a harbor light, by installing a fourth order lens in it.

A new Fort Jefferson lighthouse was built in 1876, at the top of a staircase on the fort's walls. It was a hexagonal tower 37 feet tall, and is still in good shape. It served until 1912, when the fort was closed. The moat which reportedly held sharks, now serves as a sea turtle nursery. Bring a picnic lunch and drinks.

**MUSEUM OR INTERPRETIVE SERVICE.** There is history of the fort itself, but little was found concerning the light houses.

**GETTING THERE.** There are several seaplane flights, and at least one major boat firm that goes to Fort Jefferson. Check with the Key West Chamber of Commerce for a half hour flight or a longer boat ride.

**TALES AND LEGENDS.** Dr. Samuel Mudd was a Maryland physician who innocently set the broken leg of John Wilkes Booth, Abraham Lincoln's assassin. Dr. Mudd was condemned to life imprisonment, and was sent to Fort Jefferson. He was pardoned in 1869 after performing heroically during a yellow fever epidemic at the fort. His descendants cleared his name within the past decade.

During the late 1800's and early 1900's, a naval squadron was stationed in Tortugas Harbor. The most famous ship from that squadron, the second-class battleship U.S.S. Maine, was sunk in Havana Harbor in 1898 to precipitate the Spanish-American War.

James Fenimore Cooper's novel *Jack Tier, or the Florida Reef (1848)* was set in the Garden Key lighthouse, and Ernest Hemingway's short story, *After the Storm (1932)* takes place to the east of Garden Key.

# DRY TORTUGAS LIGHTHOUSE
## (LOGGERHEAD KEY)

**HISTORY.** A lighthouse to supplement the one on Garden Key was built a mere 2.6 miles west on Loggerhead Key. It stood from 1826 to 1856, when it was toppled by a hurricane.

The new 157 ft. tall brick tower was first lighted in 1858. It held a second order fresnel lens, with a kerosene powered lantern. The 226 granite steps are imbedded in the interior brick wall and an interior brick column. The tower is half white and half black.

When it was battered by hurricanes in both 1873 and 1875, the Lighthouse Board requested money for a new tower. While awaiting funds, the tower was strengthened and the top 9 feet was rebuilt. The old tower weathered the storms so well, that the Board cancelled plans for a new tower.

The light was automated in 1986, and the classic lens were removed. Since it is unmanned and remote, there is no public access to the lighthouse. Camping by private boaters is allowed on the island.

**MUSEUM OR INTERPRETIVE SERVICE.** None.

**GETTING THERE.** Private boat or seaplane.

**TALES AND LEGENDS.** None now known.

*They stood as signals to the land,*
*Each one a lovely light.*

*Samuel Coleridge*

# GLOSSARY OF TERMS

**Argand lamp-** a lamp designed by Swiss chemist Aime' Argand. The lamp had a cylindrical wick supplied with air to the inside as well as the outside of the wick in order to expose the fuel to a maximum amount of air.

**candlepower-** luminous intensity of a light source expressed in light given by a single candle.

**encroachment-** the act of advancing or making inroads beyond the usual limits. In this book it normally refers to the sea' s advance.

**fresnel lens-** a lens designed by physicist Augustus Fresnel in 1822. The lens concentrated light rays, and greatly improved their visibility.
Lenses are classified as to size by the term "order", the first order being the largest and the sixth order the smallest. The actual size of the lens is measured by its inside diameter. The standard lens are as follows:

| ORDER | INSIDE DIAMETER | HEIGHT |
|---|---|---|
| First | 72.44 inches | 7 ft. 10 in. |
| Second | 55.12 inches | 6 ft. 1 in. |
| Third | 39.38 inches | 4 ft. 8 in. |
| Fourth | 19.69 inches | 2 ft. 4 in. |
| Fifth | 14.75 inches | 1 ft. 8 in. |
| Sixth | 11.75 inches | 1 ft. 5 in. |

**headland-** a point of land running out into the sea.

**incandescent vapor lamp-** a lamp in which air and fuel are pressurized and fed into a mantle which will not burn, is incandescent.

**lantern room-** the glassed-in enclosure at the top of a lighthouse which surrounds the lens and lamp.

61

**lighthouse leg-** a stiffness felt in the front of the thighs the day after climbing up a lighthouse. Can be avoided by stretching legs before and after.

**nominal range-** the distance from which a light can be seen on a clear night from a 30 ft. ship's bridge.

**parabolic reflector-** a reflector curved so as to concentrate light into a single beam.

**prism-** a glass device for refracting (bending) or for concentrating light, as in a lens.

**spermaceti-** a white waxy substance from the head of a sperm whale, used to make candles.

**spider lamp-** a lamp with a number of wicks installed in a single container or reservoir.

**tabby-** a building material made from equal parts of lime, shells, and gravel. Used for buildings.

**vega lantern-** an extremely bright light, named after Vega, the 4th brightest star in the entire sky.

**wickie-** a term historically used to refer to lighthouse keepers, whose job normally involved trimming the wicks of lamps in the lighthouse. Current use refers to lighthouse enthusiasts.

# SELECTED GENERAL REFERENCES

Adamson, Hans Christian, "Keepers of the Lights",
  Greenberg Publishers, N.Y., 1955.
Beaver, Patrick, "A History of Lighthouses", Peter
  Davies Publishers, London, 1971.
Dean, Love, "Reef Lights, Windswept Lighthouses of
  the Florida Keys", The Historic Key West
  Preservation Board, Key West, Fla., 1982.
Holland, Francis Ross, "America's Lighthouses, An
  Illustrated History", Dover, N.Y. 1988.
_____, "Great American Lighthouses"
  The Preservation Press,Washington,D.C.,1989.
Kochel, Kenneth G. "America's Atlantic Coast
  Lighthouses, A Traveler's Guide", Second Ed.
  Betken Publ., Clearwater, Fla., 1996.
Nordhoff, Charles(ed.), "The Lighthouses of the United
  States in 1874", Outbooks,Golden, Colo.,1981.
McCarthy, Kevin M., "Florida Lighthouses", Univ. of
  Florida Press, Gainesville, Fla., 1990.
Roberts, B. and Jones, R. " Southern Lighthouses",
  Globe Pequot Press, Chester, Conn., 1989
Stick,David, "North Carolina Lighthouses", N.C. Dept.
  of Cultural Resources, Raleigh,N.C.1988.
Strobridge, Truman R. "Chronology of Aids to
  Navigation and the Old Lighthouse Service,
  1716-1939", CG 458, Public Affairs Division,
  U.S. Coast Guard, Wash. D.C.,1974.
U.S. Coast Guard, "Historically Famous Lighthouses",
  CG 232, Department of Transportation,U.S.
  Government Printing Office,Wash., D.C. 1972.
Lighthouse Digest,P.O. Box 1690, Wells, Me.,04090
  (A monthly lighthouse magazine connected with
  the Lighthouse Depot, a great gift shop.)

# LIGHTHOUSE ORGANIZATIONS
(Send for membership information.)

## NATIONAL ORGANIZATIONS

The United States Lighthouse Society
244 Kearny St.
San Francisco, California 94108
 A non-profit historical and educational organization dedicated to lighthouse history and preservation. Sponsors lighthouse tours and publishes "The Keeper's Log" quarterly.

Lighthouse Preservation Society
P.O. Box 736
Rockport, Massachusetts, 01966
 An organization dedicated to the preservation of lighthouses throughout the United States.

## REGIONAL ORGANIZATIONS

Great Lakes Lighthouse Keepers Association
P.O. Box 580
Allen Park, Michigan 48101
 Similar to U.S.L.S. except that focus is strictly on lighthouses of the Great Lakes. Sponsors tours and publishes "The Beacon", a newsletter.

Outer Banks Lighthouse Society
301 Driftwood St.,
Nags Head, North Carolina 27959
 An organization focussing on preservation of the North Carolina lighthouses. Sponsors meetings and publishes "Lighthouse News", a newsletter.

## LOCAL LIGHTHOUSE ASSOCIATIONS

Ponce DeLeon Lighthouse Preservation Assoc., Inc.
4931 South Peninsula Drive
Ponce Inlet, Florida 32019

Coastal Georgia Historical Society
P.O. Box 21136
St. Simons Island, Georgia 31522-0636

Florida History Center and Museum
805 North U.S. Highway One
Jupiter, Florida 33477   (Jupiter Inlet Lighthouse)

Tybee Island Historical Society
P.O. Box 1334
Tybee Island, Georgia 3132

St. Augustine Lighthouse and Museum
81 Lighthouse Avenue
St. Augustine, Florida 32084

Outer Banks Conservationists,Inc.
P.O. Box 361
Corolla, North Carolina 27927 (Currituck Beach)

Key West Art and Historical Society
938 Whitehead Street
Key West, Florida 33040

Shore Village Museum         ( This is the most
104 Limerock Street            complete  lighthouse
Rockland, Maine 04841         museum we have visited.
                             Send for a newsletter.)

# INDEX

# NOTES